THE PLACE OF ANARCHISM IN SOCIALISTIC EVOLUTION

New Edition (enlarged)　　　　　　　TWO PENCE

The Place of Anarchism in Socialistic Evolution

AN ADDRESS DELIVERED IN PARIS
BY
PETER KROPOTKIN

TRANSLATED BY HENRY GLASSE

AN APPEAL TO THE
YOUNG
By Petter Kropotkin
PRICE - - - 2d.

WILLIAM REEVES　　83 CHARING CROSS ROAD,
BOOKSELLER LIMITED.　　—LONDON, W.C.2.—

ISBN: 978-1-6673-0679-7 paperback
ISBN: 978-1-6673-0680-3 hardcover

PART I.

You must often have asked yourselves what is the cause of Anarchism, and why, since there are already so many Socialist schools, it is necessary to found an additional one—that of Anarchism. In order to answer this question I will go back to the close of last century.

You all know the characteristics which marked that epoch: there was an expansion of intelligence, a prodigious development of the natural sciences, a pitiless examination of accepted prejudices, the formation of a theory of Nature based on a truly scientific foundation, observation and reasoning. In addition to these there was criticism of the political institutions bequeathed to Humanity by preceding ages, and a movement towards that ideal of Liberty, Equality, and Fraternity which has in all times been the ideal of the popular masses. Fettered in its free development by despotism and by the narrow selfishness of the privileged classes, this movement, being at the same time favoured by an explosion of popular indignation, engendered the Great Revolution which had to force its way through the midst of a thousand obstacles both without and within.

The Revolution was vanquished, but its ideas remained. Though at first persecuted and derided, they became the watchword for a whole century of slow evolution. The history of the nineteenth century is summed up in an effort to put in practice the principles elaborated at the end of last century: this is the lot of revolutions: though vanquished they establish the course of the evolution which follows them. In the domain of politics these ideas are abolition of aristocratic privileges, abolition of personal government, and equality before the law. In the economic order the Revolution proclaimed freedom of business transactions; it said—"Sell and buy freely. Sell, all of you, your products, if you can produce, and if you do not possess the implements necessary for that purpose but have only your arms to sell, sell them, sell your labour to the highest bidder, the State will not interfere! Compete among yourselves, contractors! No favour shall be shown, the law of natural selection will take upon itself the function of killing off those who do not keep pace with the progress of industry, and will reward those who take the lead."

The above is at least the *theory* of the Revolution of 1789, and if the State intervenes in the struggle to favour some to the detriment of others, as we have lately seen when the monopolies of mining and railway companies have been under discussion, such action is regarded by the liberal school as a lamentable deviation from the grand principles of the Revolution.

What has been the result? You know only too well, both women and men, idle opulence for a few and uncertainty for the morrow and misery for the greater number; crisis and wars for the conquest of markets, and a lavish expenditure of public money to find openings for industrial speculators. All this is because in proclaiming liberty of contract an essential point was neglected by our fathers. Not but what some of them caught sight of it, the best of them earnestly desired but did not dare to realise it. While liberty of transactions, that is to say a conflict between the members of society, was proclaimed, the contending parties were not equally matched, and the powerful, armed for the contest by the means inherited from their fathers, have gained the upper hand over the weak. Under such conditions the millions of poor ranged against a few rich could not do otherwise than give in.

Comrades! you have often asked yourselves —"Whence comes the wealth of the rich? Is it from their labour?" It would be a mockery to say that it was so. Let us suppose that M. Rothschild has worked all his life: well, you also, every one of you working men have also laboured: then why should the fortune of M. Rothschild be measured by hundreds of millions while your possessions are so small? The reason is simple: you have exerted yourselves to produce by your own labour, while M. Rothschild has devoted himself to accumulating the product of the labour of others—the whole matter lies in that.

But some one may say to me;—"How comes it that millions of men thus allow the Rothschilds and the Mackays to appropriate the fruit of their labour?" Alas, they cannot help themselves under the existing social system! But let us picture to our minds a city all of whose inhabitants find their lodging, clothing, food and occupation secured to them, on condition of producing things useful to the community, and let us suppose a Rothschild to enter this city bringing with him a cask full of gold. If he spends his gold it will diminish rapidly; if he locks it up it will not increase, because gold does not grow like seed, and after the lapse of a twelvemonth he will not find £110 in his drawer if he only put £100 into it. If he sets up a factory and proposes to the inhabitants of the town that they should work in it for four shillings a day while producing to the value of eight shillings a day they reply—"Among us you'll find no one willing to work on those terms. Go elsewhere and settle in some town where the unfortunate people have neither clothing, bread, nor work assured to them, and where they will consent to give up to you the lion's share of the result of their labour in return for the barest necessaries of life. Go where men starve! there you will make your fortune!"

The origin of the wealth of the rich is your misery. Let there be no poor, then we shall have no millionaires.

The facts I have just stated were such as the Revolution of last century did not comprehend or else could not act upon. That Revolution placed face to face two opposing ranks, the one consisting of a hungry, ill-clad army of former serfs, the other of men well provided with means. It then said to these two arrays—"Fight out your battle." The unfortunate were vanquished. They possessed no fortunes, but they had something more precious than all the gold in the world—their arms; and these arms, the source of all wealth, were monopolised by the wealthy. Thus we have seen those immense fortunes which are the characteristic feature of our age spring up on all sides. A king of the last century, "the great Louis the Fourteenth" of mercenary historians, would never have dreamed of possessing a fortune such as are held by those kings of the nineteenth century, the Vanderbilts and the Mackays.

On the other hand we have seen the poor reduced still more and more to toil for others, and while those who produced on their own account have rapidly disappeared, we find ourselves compelled under an ever increasing pressure to labour more and more to enrich the rich. Attempts have been made to remove these evils. Some have said—"Let us give equal instruction to all," and forthwith education has been spread abroad. Better human machines have been turned out, but these educated machines still labour to enrich others. This illustrious scientist, that renowned novelist, despite their education are still beasts of burden to the capitalist. Instruction improves the cattle to be exploited but the exploitation remains. Next, there was great talk about association, but the workers soon learned that they could not get the better of capital by associating their miseries, and those who cherished this illusion most earnestly were compelled to turn to Socialism.

Timid, at the outset, Socialism spoke at first in the name of Christian sentiment and morality: men profoundly imbued with the moral principles of Christianity—principles which it possesses in common with all other religions—came forward and said—"A Christian has no right to exploit his brethren!" But the ruling classes laughed in their faces with the reply—"Teach the people Christian resignation, tell them in the name of Christ that they should offer their left cheek to whosoever smites them on the right, then you will be welcome; as for the dreams of equality which you find in Christianity, go and meditate on your discoveries in prison."

Later on Socialism spoke in the name of Governmentalism; it said—"Since it is the special mission of the State to protect the weak against the strong, it is its duty to aid working men's associations; the State alone can enable working men to fight against capital and to oppose to capitalistic exploitation the free workshop of workers pocketing the entire value of the produce of their labour." To this the Bourgeoisie replied with grapeshot in 1848.

It was not until between twenty to thirty years later, at a time when the popular masses were invited to express their mind in the International Working Men's Association, that Socialism spoke in the name of the people, and formulating itself little by little in the Congresses of the great Association and later on among its successors, arrived at some such conclusion as the following:

All accumulated wealth is the product of the labour of all—of the present and of all preceding generations. This hall in which we are now assembled derives its value from the fact that it is situated in Paris—this magnificent city built by the labours of twenty successive generations. If this same hall were conveyed amid the snows of Siberia its value would be next to nothing. The machinery which you have invented and patented bears within itself the intelligence of five or six generations and is only possessed of value because it forms part of that immense whole that we call the progress of the nineteenth century. If you send your lace-making machine among the natives of New Guinea it will become valueless. We defy any man of genius of our times to tell us what share his intellect has had in the magnificent deductions of the book, the work of talent which he has produced! Generations have toiled to accumulate facts for him, his ideas have perhaps been suggested to him by a locomotive crossing the plains, as for elegance of design he has grasped it while admiring the Venus of Milo or the work of Murillo, and finally, if his book exercises any influence over us, it does so, thanks to all the circumstances of our civilisation.

Everything belongs to all! We defy anyone soever to tell us what share of the general wealth is due to each individual. See the enormous mass of appliances which the nineteenth century has created; behold those millions of iron slaves which we call machines, and which plane and saw, weave and spin for us, separate and combine the raw materials, and work the miracles of our times. No one has the right to monopolise any one of these machines and to say to others—"This is mine, if you wish to make use of it you must pay me a tax on each article you produce," any more than the feudal lord of the middle ages had the right to say to the cultivator—"This hill and this meadow are mine and you must pay me tribute for every sheaf of barley you bind, and on each haycock you heap up."

All belongs to everyone! And provided each man and woman contributes his and her share of labour for the production of necessary objects, they have a right to share in all that is produced by everybody.

PART II.

ALL things belong to all, and provided that men and women contribute their share of labour for the production of necessary objects, they are entitled to their share of all that is produced by the community at large. «But this is Communism,» you may say. Yes, it is Communism, but it is the Communism which no longer speaks in the name of religion or of the state, but in the name of the people. During the past fifty years a great awakening of the working-class has taken place! the prejudice in favour of private property is passing away. The worker grows more and more accustomed to regard the factory, the railway, or the mine, not as a feudal castle belonging to a lord, but as an institution of public utility which the public has the right to control. The idea of possession in common has not been worked out from the slow deductions of some thinker buried in his private study, it is a thought which is germinating in the brains of the working masses, and when the revolution, which the close of this century has in store for us, shall have hurled confusion into the camp of our exploiters, you will see that the mass of the people will demand Expropriation, and will proclaim its right to the factory, the locomotive, and the steamship.

Just as the sentiment of the inviolability of the home has developed during the latter half of our century, so also the sentiment of collective right to all that serves for the production of wealth has developed among the masses. It is a fact, and he who, like ourselves, wishes to share the popular life and follow its development, must acknowledge that this affirmation is a faithful summary of the people's aspirations. The tendency of this closing century is towards Communism, not the monastic or barrack-room Communism formerly advocated, but the free Communism which places the products reaped or manufactured in common at the disposal of all, leaving to each the liberty to consume them as he pleases in his own home.

This is the solution of which the mass of the people can most readily take hold, and it is the solution which the people demands at the most solemn epochs. In 1848 the formula "From each according to his abilities, to each according to his needs" was the one which went straight to the heart of the masses, and if they acclaimed the Republic and universal suffrage, it was because they hoped to attain to Communism through them. In 1871, also, when the people besieged in Paris desired to make a supreme effort to resist the invader, what was their demand?—That free rations should be served out to everyone. Let all articles be put into one common stock and let them be distributed according to the requirements of each. Let each one take freely of all that is abundant and let those objects which are less plentiful be distributed more sparingly and in due proportions—this is the solution which the mass of the workers understand best. This is also the system which is commonly practised in the rural districts (of France). So long as the common lands afford abundant pasture, what Commune seeks to restrict their use? When brush-wood and chestnuts are plentiful, what Commune forbids its members to take as much as they want? And when the larger wood begins to grow scarce, what course does the peasant adopt? — The allowancing of individuals.

Let us take from the common stock the articles which are abundant, and let those objects whose production is more restricted be served out in allowances according to requirements, giving preference to children and old persons, that is to say, to the weak. And, moreover, let all be consumed, not in public, but at home, according to individual tastes and in company with one's family and friends. This is the ideal of the masses.

But it is not enough to argue about, "Communism" and "Expropriation;" it is furthermore necessary to know who should have the management of the common patrimony, and it is especially on this question that different schools of Socialists are opposed to one another, some desiring authoritarian Communism, and others, like ourselves, declaring unreservedly in favour of anarchist Communism. In order to judge between these two, let us return once again to our starting point, the Revolution of last century.

In overturning royalty the Revolution proclaimed the sovereignty of the people; but, by an inconsistency which was very natural at that time, it proclaimed, not a permanent sovereignty, but an intermittent one, to be exercised at certain intervals only, for the nomination of deputies supposed to represent the people. In reality it copied its institutions from the representative government of England. The Revolution was drowned in blood, and, nevertheless, representative government became the watchword of Europe. All Europe, with the exception of Russia, has tried it, under all possible forms, from government based on a property qualification to the direct government of the little Swiss republics. But, strange to say, just in proportion as we have approached nearer to the ideal of a representative government, elected by a perfectly free universal suffrage, in that same proportion have its essential vices become manifest to us, till we have clearly seen that this mode of government is radically defective. Is it not indeed absurd to take a certain number of men from out the mass, and to entrust them with the management of *all* public affairs, saying to them, «Attend to these matters, we exonerate ourselves from the task by laying it upon you: it is for you to make laws on all manner of subjects—armaments and mad dogs, observatories and chimneys, instruction and street-sweeping: arrange these things as you please and make laws about them, since you are the chosen ones whom the people has voted capable of doing everything!» It appears to me that if a thoughtful and honest man were offered such a post, he would answer somewhat in this fashion:—

"You entrust me with a task which I am unable to fulfil. I am unacquainted with most of the questions upon which I shall be called on to legislate. I shall either have to work to some extent in the dark, which will not be to your advantage, or I shall appeal to you and summon meetings in which you will yourselves seek to come to an understanding on the questions at issue, in which case my office will be unnecessary. If you have formed an opinion and have formulated it, and if you are anxious to come to an understanding with others who have also formed an opinion on the same subject, then all you need do is to communicate with your neighbours and send a delegate to come to an understanding with other delegates on this specific question; but you will certainly reserve to yourselves the right of taking an ultimate decision; you will not entrust your delegate with the making of laws for you. This is how scientists and business men act each time that they have to come to an agreement."

But the above reply would be a repudiation of the representative system, and nevertheless it is a faithful expression of the idea which is growing everywhere since the vices of representative government have been exposed in all their nakedness. Our age, however, has gone still further, for it has begun to discuss the rights of the State and of Society in relation to the individual; people now ask to what point the interference of the State is necessary in the multitudinous functions of society.

Do we require a government to educate our children? Only let the worker have leisure to instruct himself, and you will see that, through the free initiative of parents and of persons fond of tuition, thousands of educational societies and schools of all kinds will spring up, rivalling one another in the excellence of their teaching. If we were not crushed by taxation and exploited by employers, as we now are, could we not ourselves do much better than is now done for us? The great centres would initiate progress and set the example, and you may be sure that the progress realised would be incomparably superior to what we now attain through our ministeries.—Is the State even necessary for the defence of a territory? If armed brigands attack a people, is not that same people, armed with good weapons, the surest rampart to oppose to the foreign aggressor? Standing armies are always beaten by invaders, and history teaches that the latter are to be repulsed by a popular rising alone.—While Government is an excellent machine to protect monopoly, has it ever been able to protect us against ill-disposed persons? Does it not, by creating misery, increase the number of crimes instead of diminishing them? In establishing prisons into which multitudes of men, women, and children are thrown for a time in order to come forth infinitely worse than when they went in, does not the State maintain nurseries of vice at the expense of the tax-payers? In obliging us to commit to others the care of our affairs, does it not create the most terrible vice of societies—indifference to public matters?

On the other hand, if we analyse all the great advances made in this century—our international traffic,

The Place of Anarchism in Socialistic Evolution

our industrial discoveries, our means of communication—do we find that we owe them to the State or to private enterprise? Look at the network of railways which cover Europe. At Madrid, for example, you take a ticket for St. Petersburg direct. You travel along railroads which have been constructed by millions of workers, set in motion by dozens of companies; your carriage is attached in turn to Spanish, French, Bavarian, and Russian locomotives: you travel without losing twenty minutes anywhere, and the two hundred francs which you paid in Madrid will be divided to a nicety among the companies which have combined to forward you to your destination. This line from Madrid to St. Petersburg has been constructed in small isolated branches which have been gradually connected, and direct trains are the result of an understanding which has been arrived at between twenty different companies. Of course there has been considerable friction at the outset, and at times some companies, influenced by an unenlightened egotism have been unwilling to come to terms with the others; but, I ask, was it better to put up with this occasional friction, or to wait until some Bismarck, Napoleon, or Zengis Khan should have conquered Europe, traced the lines with a pair of compasses, and regulated the despatch of the trains? If the latter course had been adopted, we should still be in the days of stage-coaches.

The network of railways is the work of the human mind proceeding from the simple to the complex by the spontaneous efforts of the parties interested, and it is thus that all the great enterprises of our age have been undertaken. It is quite true, indeed, that we pay too much to the managers of these enterprises; this is an additional reason for suppressing their incomes, but not for confiding the management of European railways to a central European government.

What thousands of examples one could cite in support of his same idea! Take all great enterprises such as the Suez Canal, the lines of Atlantic steamers, the telegraph which connects us with North and South America. Consider also that commercial organisation which enables you on rising in the morning to find bread at the baker's—that is, if you have the money to pay for it, which is not always the case now-a-days—meat at the butcher's, and all other things that you want at other shops. Is this the work of the State? It is true that we pay abominably dearly for middlemen; this is, however, an additional reason for suppressing them, but not for believing that we must entrust government with the care of providing for our feeding and clothing. If we closely scan the development of the human mind in our times we are struck by the number of associations which spring up to meet the varied requirement of the individual of our age—societies for study, for commerce, for pleasure and recreation; some of them, very small, for the propagation of a universal language or a certain method of short-hand writing; others with large arms, such as that which has recently been established for the defence of the English coast, or for the avoidance of lawsuits, and so on. To make a list of the associations which exist in Europe, volumes would be necessary, and it would be seen that there is not a single branch of human activity with which one or other does not concern itself. The State itself appeals to them in the discharge of its most important function—war; it says, "We undertake to slaughter, but we cannot take care of our victims; form a Red Cross Society to gather up the wounded on the battle-field and to take care of them."

Let others, if they will, advocate industrial barracks or the monastery of Authoritarian Communism, we declare that the tendency of society is in an opposite direction. We foresee millions and millions of groups freely constituting themselves for the satisfaction of all the varied needs of human beings—some of these groups organised by quarter, street, and house; others extending hands across the walls of cities, over frontiers and oceans. All of these will be composed of human beings who will combine freely, and after having performed their share of productive labour will meet together, either for the purpose of consumption, or to produce objects of art or luxury, or to advance science in a new direction. This is the tendency of the nineteenth century, and we follow it; we only ask to develop it freely, without any governmental interference. Individual liberty! "Take pebbles," said Fourrier, "put them into a box and shake them, and they will arrange themselves in a mosaic that you could never get by entrusting to anyone the work of arranging them harmoniously."

PART III.

NOW let me pass to the third part of my subject—the most important with respect to the future.

There is no more room for doubting that religions are going; the nineteenth century has given them their death blow. But religions—all religions—have a double composition. They contain in the first place a primitive cosmogony, a rude attempt at explaining nature, and they furthermore contain a statement of the public morality born and developed within the mass of the people. But when we throw religions overboard or store them among our public records as historical curiosities, shall we also relegate to museums the moral principles which they contain? This has sometimes been done, and we have seen people declare that as they no longer believed in the various religions so they despised morality and boldly proclaimed the maxim of bourgeois selfishness, "Everyone for himself." But a Society, human or animal, cannot exist without certain rules and moral habits springing up within it; religion may go, morality remains. If we were to come to consider that a man did well in lying, deceiving his neighbours, or plundering them when possible (this is the middle-class business morality), we should come to such a pass that we could no longer live together. You might assure me of your friendship, but perhaps you might only do so in order to rob me more easily; you might promise to do a certain thing for me, only to de-

The Place of Anarchism in Socialistic Evolution

ceive me; you might promise to forward a letter for me, and you might steal it just like an ordinary governor of a jail. Under such conditions society would become impossible, and this is so generally understood that the repudiation of religions in no way prevents public morality from being maintained, developed, and raised to a higher and ever higher standard. This fact is so striking that philosophers seek to explain it by the principles of utilitarianism, and recently Spencer sought to base the morality which exists among us upon physiological causes and the needs connected with the preservation of the race.

Let me give you an example in order to explain to you what *we* think on the matter.

A child is drowning, and four men who stand upon the bank see it struggling in the water. One of them does not stir, he is a partisan of "Each one for himself," the maxim of the commercial middle-class; this one is a brute and we need not speak of him further. The next one reasons thus: "If I save the child, a good report of my action will be made to the ruler of heaven, and the Creator will reward me by increasing my flocks and my serfs," and thereupon he plunges into the water. Is he therefore a moral man? Clearly not! He is a shrewd calculator, that is all. The third, who is an utilitarian, reflects thus (or at least utilitarian philosophers represent him as so reasoning): "Pleasures can be classed in two categories, inferior pleasures and higher ones. To save the life of anyone is a superior pleasure infinitely more intense and more durable than others; therefore I will save the child." Admitting that any man ever reasoned thus, would he not be a terrible egotist? and, moreover, could we ever be sure that his sophistical brain would not at some given moment cause his will to incline toward an inferior pleasure, that is to say, towards refraining from troubling himself? There remains the fourth individual. This man has been brought up from his childhood to feel himself *one* with the rest of humanity: from his childhood he has always regarded men as possessing interests in common: he has accustomed himself to suffer when his neighbours suffer, and to feel happy when everyone around him is happy. Directly he hears the heart-rending cry of the mother, he leaps into the water, not through reflection but by instinct, and when she thanks him for saving her child, he says, «What have I done to deserve thanks, my good woman? I am happy to see you happy; I have acted from natural impulse and could not do otherwise!»

You recognise in this case the truly moral man, and feel that the others are only egotists in comparison with him. The whole anarchist morality is represented in this example. It is the morality of a people which does not look for the sun at midnight—a morality without compulsion or authority, a morality of habit. Let us create circumstances in which man shall not be led to deceive nor exploit others, and then by the very force of things the moral level of humanity will rise to a height hitherto unknown. Men are certainly not to be moralised by teaching them a moral catechism: tribunals and prisons do not diminish vice; they pour it over society in floods. Men are to be moralised only by placing them in a position which shall contribute to develop in them those habits which are social, and to weaken those which are not so. A morality which has become instinctive is the true morality, the only morality which endures while religions and systems of philosophy pass away.

Let us now combine the three preceding elements, and we shall have Anarchy and its place in Socialistic Evolution.

Emancipation of the producer from the yoke of capital; production in common and free consumption of all the products of the common labour.

Emancipation from the governmental yoke; free development of individuals in groups and federations; free organisation ascending from the simple to the complex, according to mutual needs and tendencies.

Emancipation from religious morality; free morality, without compulsion or authority, developing itself from social life and becoming habitual.

The above is no dream of students, it is a conclusion which results from an analysis of the tendencies of modern society: Anarchist Communism is the union of the two fundamental tendencies of our society—a tendency towards economic equality, and a tendency towards political liberty. So long as Communism presented itself under an authoritarian form, which necessarily implies government, armed with much greater power than that which it possesses to-day, inasmuch as it implies economic in addition to political power—so long as this was the case, Communism met with no sufficient response. Before 1848 it could, indeed, sometimes excite for a moment the enthusiasm of the worker who was prepared to submit to any all-powerful government, provided it would release him from the terrible situation in which he was placed, but it left the true friends of liberty indifferent.

Anarchist Communism maintains that most valuable of all conquests—individual liberty—and moreover extends it and gives it a solid basis—economic liberty—without which political liberty in delusive; it does not ask the individual who has rejected god, the universal tyrant, god the king, and god the parliament, to give unto himself a god more terrible than any of the preceding—god the Community, or to abdicate upon its altar his independence, his will, his tastes, and to renew the vow of asceticism which he formerly made before the crucified god. It says to him, on the contrary, "No society is free so long as the individual is not so! Do not seek to modify society by imposing upon it an authority which shall make everything right; if you do, you will fail as popes and emperors have failed. Modify society so that your fellows may not be any longer your enemies by the force of circumstances: abolish the conditions which allow some to monopolise the fruit of the labour of others; and instead of attempting to construct society from top to bottom, or from the centre to the circumference, let it develop itself freely from the simple to the composite, by the free union of free groups. This course, which is so much obstructed at present, is the true forward march of society: do not seek to hinder it, do not turn your back on progress, but march along with it! Then the sentiment of sociability which is common to human beings, as it is to all animals living in society, will be able to develop itself freely, because our fellows will no longer be our enemies, and we shall thus arrive at a state of things in which each individual will be able to give free rein to his inclinations, and even to his passions, without any other restraint than the love and respect of those who surround him."

This is our ideal, and it is the ideal which lies deep in the hearts of peoples—of all peoples. We know full well that this ideal will not be attained without violent shocks; the close of this century has a formidable revolution in store for us: whether it begins in France, Germany, Spain, or Russia, it will be an European one, and spreading with the same rapidity as that of our fathers, the heroes of 1848, it will set all Europe in a blaze. This coming Revolution will not aim at a mere change of government, but will have a social character; the work of expropriation will commence, and exploiters will be driven out. Whether we like it or not, this will be done independently of the will of individuals, and when hands are laid on private property we shall arrive at Communism, because we shall be forced to do so. Communism, however, cannot be either authoritarian or parliamentary, it must either be anarchist or non-existent; the mass of the people does not desire to trust itself again to any saviour, but will seek to organise itself by itself.

We do not advocate Communism and Anarchy because we imagine men to be better than they really are; if we had angels among us we might be tempted to entrust to them the task of organising us, though doubtless even *they* would show the cloven foot very soon. But it is just because we take men as they are that we say: «Do not entrust them with the governing of you. This or that despicable minister might have been an excellent man if power had not been given to him. The only way of arriving at harmony of interests is by a society without exploiters and without rulers.» It is precisely because men are not angels that we say, «Let us arrange matters so that each man may see his interest bound up with the interests of others, then you will no longer have to fear his evil passions.»

Anarchist Communism being the inevitable result of existing tendencies, it is towards this ideal that we must direct our steps, instead of saying, "Yes, Anarchy is an excellent ideal," and then turning our backs upon it. Should the approaching revolution not succeed in realising the whole of this ideal, still all that shall have been effected in the direction of it will remain; but all that shall have been done in a contrary direction will be doomed to disappear. It is a general rule that a popular revolution may be vanquished, but that, nevertheless, it furnishes a motto for the evolution of the succeeding century. France expired under the heel of the allies in 1815, and yet the action of France had rendered serfdom impossible of continuance, all over Europe, and representative government inevitable; universal suffrage was drowned in blood, and yet universal suffrage is the watchword of the century. In 1871 the Commune expired under volleys of grapeshot, and yet the watchword in France to-day is "the Free Commune." And if Anarchist Communism is vanquished in the coming revolution, after having asserted itself in the light of day, not only will it leave behind it the abolition of private property, not only will the working man have learned his true place in society, not only will the landed and mercantile aristocracy have received a mortal blow, but Communist Anarchism will be the goal of the evolution of the twentieth century.

Anarchist Communism sums up all that is most beautiful and most durable in the progress of humanity; the sentiment of justice, the sentiment of liberty, and solidarity or community of interest. It guarantees the free evolution, both of the individual and of society. Therefore, it will triumph.

Printed by THE NEW TEMPLE PRESS,
Norbury, London, Great Britain.

www.ingramcontent.com/pod-product-compliance
Lightning Source LLC
Chambersburg PA
CBHW061316040426
42444CB00010B/2677